Gary Paulsen

WHO WROTE THAT?

Gary Paulsen

Elizabeth Paterra

Chelsea House Publishers
Philadelphia

CHELSEA HOUSE PUBLISHERS

EDITOR IN CHIEF Sally Cheney
DIRECTOR OF PRODUCTION Kim Shinners
CREATIVE MANAGER Takeshi Takahashi
MANUFACTURING MANAGER Diann Grasse

STAFF FOR GARY PAULSEN

ASSOCIATE EDITOR Benjamin Kim
PICTURE RESEARCHER Sarah Bloom, Jaimie Winkler
PRODUCTION ASSISTANT Jaimie Winkler
COVER AND SERIES DESIGNER Keith Trego
LAYOUT 21st Century Publishing and Communications, Inc.

http://www.chelseahouse.com

First Printing

1 3 5 7 9 8 6 4 2

Library of Congress Cataloging-in-Publication Data

Paterra, Elizabeth.
   Gary Paulsen / Elizabeth Paterra.
      p. cm. — (Who wrote that?)
Summary: A biography of an author whose varied experiences provided background
for many of his adventure stories, historical novels, sports books, and nature stories.
Includes bibliographical references and index.
   ISBN 0-7910-6723-8 (hardcover)
   1. Paulsen, Gary—Juvenile literature. 2. Authors, American—20th century—
Biography—Juvenile literature. 3. Adventure and adventurers—United States—
Biography—Juvenile literature. 4. Children's stories—Authorship—Juvenile
literature. 5. Wilderness areas—Juvenile literature. [1. Paulsen, Gary. 2. Authors,
American.] I. Title. II. Series.
PS3566.A834 Z826 2002
813'.54—dc21
                                                            2002001603

Table of Contents

A musher driving his team during the Iditarod in 1996. Gary Paulsen ran this 1500-mile dogsled race across Alaska for the first time in 1983, and while he didn't win, the experience itself made a huge impact on his life and was the subject of more than a few books, including Woodsong.

1

The Iditarod

GARY PAULSEN DUCKED his head and hunched his shoulders against the biting cold as he angled his sled on the trail leaving downtown Anchorage. It was a windy, blustery March day in 1983, and he was on the first leg of the Iditarod, a 1500-mile dogsled race across the freezing ice and snow of Alaska. Why would he enter such a race when he recognized the madness of it? The answer was simple: he was going for the prize money. It would be more money than Paulsen ever had, and with it, he could save his family from poverty.

Racers—known as "mushers" in dogsledding jargon—and

their dogs had to be prepared to undertake such a race as this. Paulsen knew that. So he had been training for this race for more than ten years by running traps in Northern Minnesota. As a trapper, Paulsen set snares to catch and kill small animals like beaver, fox, and rabbits. Then he skinned them and sold their furs. Sometimes the traps were set several miles apart, so Paulsen used a team of dogs to run with his sled from one trap to another. He loved his dogs and worked hard to train them as a team. He also loved to drive the dogsled and felt at home in the ice and snow.

Paulsen started his career as a dogsled runner in the mid-1970s when the state of Minnesota paid hunters to trap and skin small animals. He supported his family with the money he made. By the late 1970s, however, killing animals for their fur was no longer popular and Paulsen's trap-running business failed. But his love of training and caring for the dogs remained strong.

Paulsen first learned of the Iditarod from stories of the famous dogsled run to Nome that took place in February of 1925. At that time, a diptheria epidemic threatened the small goldmining community on the Bering Sea. The people, especially the children, needed life-saving serum. Airplanes at the time were too light and fragile to fly the distance from Anchorage to Nome in the middle of winter so they could not be used. And the Alaskan Train service that started in 1914 did not extend the full distance. So the federal government constructed a winter trail for dogsled teams. Musher teams of dogsleds—pulled by 12 to 20 huskies—worked in relays, with each musher delivering to the next stop along the way.

By the early 1940s, snowmobiles, better airplanes, and increased train service replaced dogsleds. As a result, dogsledding remained only as a celebrated and daring athletic event. Dogsled running was Paulsen's way of life and he was proud of his skills, so he was determined to use them to win the Iditarod.

Paulsen was also an established writer by the late 1970s. He wrote articles and books with titles like *Dribbling, Shooting and Scoring Sometimes, Remodeling a Used Comprehensive Home and Shelter Book*, and *Careers in an Airport*. Even though his published pieces sold well, he was making no more than $3,000 a year. Without his trapping business, his family would live in poverty. He thought the answer to his problems lay in winning the prize money from the Iditarod. But he had one other avenue to try—writing fiction based on aspects of his own life.

Recalling his experiences when he visited the Philippines in 1945 and as a serviceman in 1957, he turned them into stories. One of his first books was *Foxman*, the story of a World War II veteran and fox trapper who suffered from a badly-scarred face. His next book was *Winterkill*, which told the story of an alcoholic family. Since Paulsen grew up in an alcoholic family and later became an alcoholic himself, he knew the situation well. However, the reaction to *Winterkill* from his reading public was disastrous. People thought they recognized themselves in *Winterkill* and sued him. After months of haggling among the lawyers, his case moved to the Supreme Court where he eventually won— but Paulsen was left bankrupt and bitter.

Richard Jackson, then editor-in-chief at Bradbury Press, was familiar with Paulsen's books and admired his writing style. He called Paulsen to find out what he was currently writing. Paulsen answered, "I'm not writing anything. I'm running dogs and don't have money for the Iditarod!"

At that point, Jackson and Paulsen made a deal. If Jackson sent Paulsen money to get a team of dogs and a

As a writer, Paulsen thrives on real-life adventure and experience. Paulsen's own experiences as a serviceman inspired his book **Foxman.**

sled ready and paid Paulsen's entrance fee for the Iditarod, Paulsen would give Jackson and Bradbury Press the rights to publish Paulsen's next book. They both envisioned a book about running the Iditarod as a bestseller.

So it was on that cold mid-January day in 1983 that thoughts of actually running the Iditarod and making the thousands of dollars as a winner were foremost in Paulsen's mind. He also knew that running a 1500-mile race through the freezing ice and heavy snows across Alaska in January would seem crazy to most people. Nevertheless, Paulsen completed his preparations and tracked to Anchorage to begin the race.

The mushers lined up and the dogs pulled at their harnesses, anxious to begin. Paulsen took a minute to check his competition. He counted thirty-two mushers ahead of him—well-equipped teams with strong healthy dogs. He swallowed, straightened his jacket and placed his left foot on his sled. He thought about how he had first run his dogs ten miles, then fifty miles, and eventually hundreds of miles to build them as a team and give himself the discipline he needed. He reminded himself that he was well-prepared and his equipment was sturdy. He planned to win. And he had brought his notebook to record every detail.

In his award-winning book *Woodsong*, published by Puffin in 1990, Paulsen wrote about the suffering and accidents he endured even while training. He described a time when he shot off the edge of a canyon and caught himself on a sharp branch, tearing his kneecap. Paulsen assumed the dogs would run on as they usually did, and tried to crawl to the top of the canyon, but slid down and dropped into a waterfall, further injuring himself. Thinking he was abandoned, he was surprised when his lead dog, Olaf, peered over the edge, and whimpered. Paulsen encouraged her and she pulled the team around so he could crawl back on the sled and make it home. Such heroism was possible because of the mutual trust Paulsen and his team of dogs had for one another.

However, the actual Iditarod run was quite different from Paulsen's preparation runs in Minnesota. He tracked his race over seventeen days. Throughout the course of the race, Paulsen faced severe perils such as frostbite, intense cold, blinding snowstorms, hallucinations, and lost trails.

Day 1 was stamped with a false beginning. Just thirty miles out of town in the suburb of Eagle River, the dogs were stopped and loaded into trucks that would take them eleven miles to Settler's Bay, where the true race started. Of course they objected, as they were trained to run on ice and snow, not ride in trucks—imagine how they barked and whimpered. Once they stepped off the trucks and found their places along the tug line, the dogs settled into their run. Paulsen admired the fury of the snow as it spread and separated around them, like spray from a ship cutting across ocean current. Then he felt his sled settle smoothly on the trail as the dogs pushed ahead. Paulsen relaxed into the race, enjoying the team's energy and his feeling of oneness with them.

Suddenly, the dogs came to a halt and the sled stopped. Paulsen peered around to see what had happened. A huge moose was blocking his way. His lead dog stood with its nose between the legs of the foreboding creature. The moose was spooked and so were the dogs.

In *Woodsong*, Paulsen tells how the musher behind him yelled at him to kick the moose in the flank. Paulsen had always thought of moose as not only large, but essentially crazy. They not only hated dogs, but the sleds and the mushers as well. If the moose turned on him, the race was essentially over. Paulsen sneaked toward the moose. His legs shook as he leveled a blow to the moose's hindquarters. Much to his relief, the moose got the message and ambled away. Already a potentially hazardous encounter had been averted—and it was only the first day of the race.

From then on the trip was punctuated with scheduled

One of Paulsen's obstacles on his Iditarod run came in the form of a moose who blocked the way of the trail. One false move and the moose could have turned on Paulsen and his dogs and dashed their hopes for finishing the race.

stopping points along the trail. These points were located where the thriving 1900s gold rush towns had been, where dogsleds had carried away millions of dollars in gold. Now that the mines were dried up, the area was scarcely populated and services were limited.

Throughout his first Iditarod run, Paulsen cared for the

twenty dogs on his team. Twelve were harnessed to the sled and six followed along behind to be used when any of twelve fell ill or showed signs of fatigue. The dogs could get fussy and needed attention. He fed them three times a day, rubbed their shoulders every hour or so, gave them between-meal snacks, allowed them time to relieve themselves, changed their booties hundreds of times, yelled commands and pushed, constantly striving to maintain the rhythm of the run. There were even occasions when one of the dogs preferred the meat and cereal mixture Paulsen had for himself—so he went hungry in order to keep the dog satisfied. When Paulsen fell ill, he was at the mercy of the dogs. They were his caretakers. Caring for the dogs and being cared for by them became an endless routine, one that could not be interrupted unless you gave up. He wrote down his impressions and anecdotes of the dogs and other mushers he met.

He also recorded tales of his own hallucinations that came from near-starvation, cold, and lack of sleep. Although the actual race was just seventeen days, Paulsen said the trip seemed to take years.

"I'd done it in winter when the road was solid packed ice. (It) was always dark and I couldn't honestly remember a single bit of the drive except for the endless routine of taking dogs out to let them piss and feeding them and watering them and driving another three hours and doing it all again."

In *Woodsong*, Paulsen wrote that every part of the Iditarod is intense. He said that there is a point when the musher and his dogs find themselves all alone in the vastness of Alaska. He described this as the "start-madness" that really pulls the musher and his dogs together so they become one as a team. Imagine weather so cold and wind so strong you feel your eyelids leave their sockets and find snow deposited on your eyeballs.

Paulsen considered his first race in 1983 to be a success, even though it was a harrowing experience. He did not win, but he made it from Anchorage to Safety, the last check-in point. Most importantly, his team was safe—he did not lose any of the dogs.

So he tried it again in 1984. This time his route was a more northerly one. The checkpoint towns were Cripple, Ruby, Galena, and Nulato. But he lost his way and never reached Nome. His dogs scattered down an ice hill near Galena and had to be rescued by a helicopter. Paulsen wrote about his suffering through the "cut and grind" of the storms, saying, "What made it all worth the efforts (along with finding the love that comes from dogs) was the country." 1984 was Gary Paulsen's last try at the Iditarod, but certainly not his last adventure. When he was 57 years old, he purchased a Harley-Davidson motorcycle and tracked over the route he had taken as a dogsledder in the Iditarod. And he wrote many books based on his experiences in Alaska. He gloried in Eskimo traditions and how their way of life harmonized with nature.

Throughout his life, Paulsen has been a carpenter, an explorer, an engineer, a soldier, a hunter, a trapper, a migrant worker, a dreamer, a boat captain, a husband, a father, and an alcoholic. Paulsen's books for young people are filled with songs, memories, joy, and frustration from his experiences. He relives his life as he writes his books.

He is also very aware of the lives of teenagers today. One day his sixteen-year-old son Jim talked to him about being afraid of dying young. Paulsen remembers asking him, "What are you scared of?"

His son answered, "The nuclear thing."

An aerial view of the Cripple checkpoint of the Iditarod race. Paulsen doesn't mince words about the brutality of the cold and isolation of the race, but also notes how it bonds the musher with his dogs and truly makes them a team.

"OK, well we got to do something about it," Paulsen replied.

He sat down with his son and they wrote a letter to Russia. "Dear Russia," it read, "We don't want to kill you and we don't want you to kill us. Gary Paulsen and his son Jim do not want to blow you up and we do not want you to blow us up."

After this, Paulsen determined to write books that posed

problems and asked questions, instead of giving lectures or suggesting solutions as conventional stories do. His characters are based on real people. And he doesn't excuse adults for their role in causing world disasters. In 1986, he wrote *Sentries*, a book about the lives of four very different teenagers who face hard problems and who recognize adults cannot help them.

Using his special gifts as a writer of fast-paced adventures and death-defying survival stories, Paulsen never offers moral lessons. He simply tells stories that give the reader experiences they can use as they face problems in their own time and place.

Iditarod Glossary

BASKET—bed of the sled

BOOTIES—Cashmere socks to protect dog's paws.

GEE—tells the team to turn left

HAW—tells the team to turn right

DOUBLE LEAD—two dogs lead the team side by side

LEAD DOG—dog at head of team, must know commands

IDITAROD—distant place

MUSH—tells team to go

"ON-BY"—musher yells to pass another sled

SWING DOG—dog right behind the lead dog

TEAM DOGS—dogs who pull the sled

TUG LINE—rope connecting the dogs' harnesses

WHEEL DOGS—dogs closest to sled

Gary and his mother Eunice spent the early 1940's in Chicago while his father Oscar was abroad with the military.

2

Mother and Son

GARY PAULSEN WAS born May 17, 1939 in Minneapolis, in the northern part of Minnesota. Shortly after Gary's birth, his father, Oscar, left home to become a career military officer and served under General George Patton in France and Germany. Eunice, Gary's mother, moved with her infant son to Chicago where she worked alternating night and day shifts in a munitions factory making airplanes, guns, and shells. Clara was the babysitter who cared for Gary when his mother was on night shift. Clara adored Jack Benny and Red Skelton, two radio and TV comedians who were popular in the 1940's and 50's. He and Clara would laugh at their jokes and sing their songs over and over along with the radio.

Because of the strange hours of her night shift schedule, Eunice and Gary would take afternoon naps together. Once, when he was five years old, he thought his mother was asleep and he slipped out of the apartment to see what it was like to be on his own. Wandering down an alleyway near his house, he was stopped by a boisterous man, dressed in tattered clothes. He was huge and frightening to the young boy. No sooner had the man reached out to grab Gary than the man was knocked over by a blow to his head. Gary's mother had awakened, found Gary missing and went to look for him. When she saw the man with his hands on Gary, she hit the man on the head so hard that he dropped the boy. Before she moved to hit him a second time, she yelled at Gary to run home as quickly as he could. Eunice had saved her son from a child molester.

Realizing the potential danger of leaving him alone, Gary's mother would take Gary to taverns with her. Dressed in a miniature army uniform, Gary would entertain anyone who listened to him. He said his father was off at war, killing the bad Germans. Then, while sitting at the bar, he would sing songs like "Mairzy Doats" or "Itty Bitty Fishes," which were popular songs in the 1940's. He was such a novelty to the patrons at the tavern that they often bought him dinner.

These good times couldn't mask the absence of Gary's father in his life. Gary remembers a letter his mother received from his father one day. His mother cried and hugged Gary, but did not fully explain why the letter upset her, only that his father had a new "friend" in France. He found out later that this actually meant that his father had a new girlfriend.

After this, Eunice had a hard time paying bills because Oscar was not sending them money regularly. By this time, Eunice was drinking and had a boyfriend named Casey. Gary did not mind that his mother had a boyfriend, but he was distressed when Casey moved into their apartment. Eunice suggested that Gary call Casey "Uncle Casey." This did not make Gary feel any better. He would silently think of saying to Casey, "Sure you can smile at me, but I hate you and I hope the krauts (Germans) or nips (Japanese) or maybe my father comes and kills you."

During summers when Gary was not in school, he spent his vacations with his grandmother and his cousins in Minnesota. There he began to build his memories of hunting and life on the farm. Experiences from these summers are reflected in *Winter Room*. In this Newbery Honor Book of 1989, the first-person narrator lives on a farm with his older brother Wayne and their Uncle David, who was "So old we don't even know for sure how old he is." The book recounts farm tasks of the seasons, planting, looking after the animals, Saturday evening dances in the summer, and slaughtering steer and chickens for winter food. It also brings out the character of Uncle David, who tells stories around the winter fire. Uncle David sits rocking in his chair as he starts his story with, "It was when I was young. . . ." There is hurt in Uncle David's eyes as he speaks. After telling the story Uncle David gets up to prove he is still the man he used to be. Going out to the woodpile, he uses two sharp axes to split a log exactly down the middle, just as he had done when he was a young man. Following this show of bravado, Uncle David again resigns himself to his quiet life.

After his summers in northern Minnesota, Gary returned home to Chicago to live with his mother during the school year. School was never pleasant for Gary. Reading did not come easily to him and he did not relate well to the other children. Eunice loved her son, but she was not always home to show interest in his schoolwork or to read to him. His attendance was poor and he did not do well in his studies.

In August 1945, when World War II was coming to its end, things changed for Gary. Over the next six months, Eunice received two or three letters from Oscar every day. This had a positive effect on her, and she not only cut back on her drinking but also paid more attention to her son. Sitting at the kitchen table, Eunice would read Oscar's letters aloud to Gary. She would brew fresh coffee for herself and give Gary a cup of Ovaltine. Then she would open the letters, fold the creases back, and smooth them out, smiling as she read parts of the letters aloud. These times spent sharing Oscar's letters became a cherished routine. Gary felt pride when Eunice told him that Oscar had done well in the service and that now he was known as *Officer* Paulsen.

In one of the letters that Eunice received, Oscar wrote that since the war was formally over, he had been reassigned to the Philippine Islands to help with the rebuilding of the government there. He had written, "You and the boy will be getting travel vouchers in a day or two and you will proceed to San Francisco where you will find a ship waiting to take you to the Philippines . . . I'll see you in Manila."

Gary and his mother began their journey the next day. When they reached the train station in Chicago, they saw families rushing to meet discharged sons, husbands, and sweethearts. It was so crowded that Eunice gripped Gary's hand as well as their bags to keep from losing him. In turn, Gary cuddled Dog, his stuffed animal, under his

A 1950's Ovaltine ad evoking feelings of warmth and safety. Gary would drink Ovaltine while his mother read letters from his father aloud, which became a kind of tradition between the two of them.

arm tightly, as he did not want to lose his best friend.

From Chicago, they traveled as far as Minneapolis. At that point they were stopped. The trains were filled. Gary and his mother would have to wait four days before they could continue. The trip from Minneapolis to San

Francisco would take several more days. In *Eastern Sun, Winter Moon*, Paulsen explains that what made it even worse was that they needed to reach San Francisco within the next seven days or they would miss their ship to Manila.

A discharged serviceman was attracted to Eunice's beauty. When he saw her dilemma, he asked Eunice if she would be willing to help him drive from Minneapolis to San Fransciso. He said they could alternate drivers so one person could sleep while the other one drove. This way they would make it to San Francisco in time. Gary's mother hesitated only briefly before she agreed. The serviceman was quite pleased to think Eunice would be traveling with him. Once the trip was underway, however, Eunice let the serviceman know she was not interested in anything except getting to San Francisco in time to board the ship to Manila.

Japan and America at war

When World War II began in Europe in 1939, Japanese armies occupied French Indochina. By 1940, Japan strengthened its alliance with Germany and Italy, and by 1941, Japan was at war with the United States.

Japan's first major defeat occurred in May, 1942, when the United States won the Battle of the Coral Sea. In 1945, U.S. bombers pounded the cities, and American submarines cut off shipping and transport of vital supplies to Japan. On August 6, the United States dropped the first atomic bomb to be used in warfare on the city of Hiroshima.

It was a difficult trip for a six-year-old to make. Not many 1940 sedans were air-conditioned and Gary felt confined as he wiggled around in the back seat. The land was hot and dry for the first two days but Gary did not complain. He soon found out that stops, however, would only be for eating. When Gary needed to go to the bathroom, he had to use an old coffee can when riding in the car. At first he thought this was funny, but he soon got tired of it. By the end of the third day they reached snow-capped mountains and were glad of the cooler weather.

Then a new misfortune threatened their trip. Gary was sick to his stomach, throwing up and running a fever. Two days later as they drove into the city of San Francisco, Gary noticed little red spots all over his body. When the spots turned into bumps and became itchy, Eunice knew he had chicken pox. Eunice was afraid Gary would not be allowed on the ship. So when they finally reached the dock where the boat was moored, Eunice took Gary to the doctor. Gary's disease was confirmed. Nevertheless, the doctor felt it was safe to give Gary the shots he needed to protect him from malaria and other diseases prevalent in the Philippines. Gary stayed at a small hotel while his mother met with Captain Pederson, the captain of the ship. Eunice told Gary that she and Captain Pederson would discuss ways to sneak Gary aboard, in spite of his red spots.

Soon Eunice and the captain developed a plan for slipping Gary aboard. The plan was to hustle Gary into a stateroom on the ship without any of the port authorities knowing. His mother said he would be there alone for the rest of the night and the next day. She and the captain wrapped Gary in a Navy blanket. The coarseness of the blanket bothered his sore skin, but he knew it would not be for long. He hugged Dog close to him. Gary did not mind being alone, for he knew that his mother would be back for him as soon as she could.

The next day, a sailor carried Gary to the ship's infirmary and tucked him into a white hospital bed. His mother, along with the ship's doctor, checked on him each day. Sailors also visited him, bringing him candy, comic books and soda. Gary knew the sailors came to his room so they could meet his mother—everywhere they went, sailors and soldiers gathered around them, asking his mother her name and if she would like to have a date with them. After nine days in the infirmary, Gary's spots disappeared and the ship's doctor declared him well again. He was finally free to enjoy life on the ship.

Gary enjoyed strolling the deck with his arm linked with his mother's, enjoying the breezes and admiring the clear sky and the white caps as the waves slashed up against the ship. One day, however, while they watched the horizon, a silver plane flashed across in the sunlight. Its flight pattern looked crazy to Gary. Then it crashed. Servicemen from throughout the boat crowded to the deck, hugging the railing, watching helplessly. First the tail dropped off. Then the body of the plane began to sink. Women and children passengers, many of them relatives of servicemen, poured out of the plane. There were so many people that rescue boats could not reach everyone, and a lot of them fell into the sea.

The captain ordered rescue boats to gather the wounded and bring them back to the ship. Gary heard the children crying and saw that many of them were badly hurt. Eunice told Gary to stay out of the way while she helped administer first aid to those in need.

The attack on Pearl Harbor happened on December 7, 1941, but the war's effects were still apparent in Honolulu by the time Gary and his mother passed through in 1945.

For the next eighteen hours, Eunice helped distribute medicine and make the crash victims as comfortable as she could. Gary remembers seeing spots of blood that spilled on the deck. When he went back to his cabin, he saw two little terribly injured young girls in his bunk. One of the girls was holding Dog, and Gary noticed that Dog had been stained with her blood. Gary decided to let them sleep and perhaps give up Dog to them as well.

The next part of their trip was from Honolulu, the capital city of Hawaii. The ship was anchored several miles from shore and met by a passenger barge. The barge would take the victims of the accident to land where they would get hospital care. Gary and his mother traveled in the barge with them. A Navy tugboat guided the barge into dock.

Military ships and fishing boats surrounded them as they made their way to shore, and they were greeted by servicemen stationed in the Philippines and by the Hawaiian natives. Gary saw a destroyer, a submarine, an aircraft carrier, and several smaller ships. The signs of war were all around them. Paulsen remembers that "everything seemed blown to pieces." In contrast to the sights, he delighted in the smells wafting through the air. To him, the air had a new thickness to it, like it was filled with blooming flowers and green foliage.

After two days in Honolulu, Gary and his mother boarded another ship bound for Okinawa. This trip was almost twice as far as their trip from San Francisco to Honolulu. When they arrived in Okinawa, a soldier carrying a submachine gun walked up to them. He introduced himself as Officer Ryland, Officer Paulsen's assistant. He explained to Eunice that he had been sent by Oscar to fetch her and Gary. Gary noted that his manner seemed to bother his mother—she even said to him, "I think your manner is insolent." But Gary and Eunice had no choice in the matter. They climbed in the jeep, driven by the unfriendly gunner. Eunice gave a nickel to each of the Filipinos who loaded their luggage in the back seat.

The jeep made its way through Manila. Gary and Eunice stared at craters where bombs had wiped out

Retreating Japanese forces left Manila in ruins, and the sights were even more horrifying to Gary and his mother up close in real life as they approached their new home.

shopping centers, homes and buildings. Native Filipinos dug through the trash and debris, weeping for lost family and neighbors. Even though Gary and Eunice had seen pictures of this devastation on TV at home, seeing it with their own eyes made the horror real to them.

Gary and his mother reached the war-torn city of Manila to reunite with Gary's father Sergeant Oscar Paulsen at the military base where he was stationed. Life would prove to be very different in the Philippines from what Gary was used to in the United States.

3

Family Life in the Philippines

THE JEEP FINALLY reached the military base where Gary and his family would spend the next two years. Up ahead, he saw houses built on stilts standing at least three feet off the ground. To Gary, the walls looked like matting woven from strips of bamboo.

Eunice cried out in surprise. There would be almost no privacy, she said, exclaiming "You can see right through the walls." There were more surprises for Gary and his mother when they arrived at their new home in the Philippines. All the houses on the army base looked alike, appearing to be too flimsy to be real homes. They were all in a row and balanced on stilts. Gary thought they looked like paper cutouts.

Sergeant Ryland brought the jeep to a stop on the gravel street in front of house Number 26. Gary ran up and across the porch into their new home. Inside, Gary noted that the house had two bedrooms, a kitchen, and a bathroom. He saw that the bathroom was the only room with a door. Coming back into the living room, he looked carefully at the walls. They were made of mesh, like a net, with a screen. Then his glance went to the ceiling that was lined with exposed wood beams—as well as other things.

The seven-year-old yanked on his mother's slacks and pointed up. "Look at the ceiling," he said. "It's got lizards . . . "

Gary remembers his mother yelling, then she grabbed a broom and swatted at the creatures. Some dropped on the floor, and some landed in her hair. Others ran back up the wall. Eunice ran to the kitchen sink to remove the lizards that had gotten in her hair before she ran back out to attack the rest of the lizards.

At that moment, someone yelled "What in hell are you doing?" and a tall, handsome man stepped into the living room. Gary saw he was wearing khakis and his hair was black and wavy. When his mother introduced the man as his father, Gary was stunned. Like the images of the war he had seen before, he could scarcely believe it when was finally in the presence of his father, recognizing him from the pictures he had seen.

Gary stood transfixed, unable to move. At the same time, Eunice flew over to Oscar. They embraced and he tilted her chin back and kissed her. Right away Eunice began to apologize for her tangled hair. Gary did not move until his mother took his hand and led him toward his father. When his father asked for a hug, Gary lifted his arms to him. His father lifted him up and hugged Gary. Finally, his shyness disappearing, he stammered, "We came on a ship," and started talking breathlessly about the things they had gone through. His father laughed and told him that they would have plenty of time to talk later.

Gary could hardly believe he finally had a real father. Gary checked his own image in the bathroom mirror. He wanted to be sure that he and his father were related. But Gary's hair was blond, almost white, not dark and wavy like his father's. How could he possibly be related to that tall, dark-haired man? Furthermore, it was hard for the seven-year-old to get used to the idea of having a real father, someone who would love him.

On top of that, Gary would have a bedroom of his own. Now that his father was here, Oscar would be sharing the room where his mother slept. Looking at his own bed, Gary saw that it was covered with netting. His mother explained that netting would keep the mosquitoes off of him when he was asleep. She told him these were the mosquitoes that carried the dreaded malaria disease.

Oscar sat down and talked with Eunice while she unpacked and cleaned the house. Gary heard his father say, "You won't have to do any housework. Tomorrow the housegirl and boy will be here, and they will take over the household duties." Housegirl and houseboy were the names used for the Filipino servants who worked for the officer's families, Oscar explained. Their names were Rom and Maria and even though he referred to them as "houseboy" and "housegirl," they were actually in their twenties.

His father said that Sergeant Ryland, the rude military official who had driven then to the compound, would supply their food. "I don't want to see him again," Eunice burst out.

Oscar stood tall, assuming a patient pose. His voice was flat. "You'll have to change, have to understand . . . " he said, and he kissed her again.

Using the same, military, flat voice, he used when he told Eunice about the house servants, he said to Gary, "There are rules. You cannot leave the housing compound alone." He told Gary that a cannon sounded every day at five o'clock and Gary had to be in the house with his hands washed for dinner at that time, or else he would be restricted. This meant he would not be allowed to leave the house. With that Officer Paulsen left his wife and son and joined Ryland in the jeep.

Eunice fixed lunch, their first meal in the new house. She found a can of Spam and made sandwiches. Gary did not care for the saltiness of the meat and went to the kitchen sink for a drink of water. He screamed when a river of black, angry-looking ants streamed out of the faucet. One of them bit Gary's outstretched hand. Eunice grabbed him and brushed the ants away. Then she reached for bug spray and killed every one of them. After that, Eunice found a broom and thoroughly cleaned while Gary looked at old magazine pictures of war-torn Hawaii and Manila that Eunice had brought with them. He and his mother agreed that they were living in the midst of horror created by war.

Gary found out that the Filipino servants who served the families in the compound had a reputation as thieves. When they stole money or even bottles of Coke, they were often beaten mercilessly by the people they worked for.

But the Filipinos took the beatings without complaining, as it was the price they willingly paid for goods to take home to their families that lived outside of the compound. Gary found out later that both Maria's and Rom's families were so poor that they depended on handouts from the military for their survival.

When Maria and Rom took over the cleaning and cooking, Eunice found she had time on her hands with nothing to do. She began spending her days visiting with the other wives, playing bridge, and drinking. Soon Gary got used to the way of life in the compound. Since he was left on his own, with no other children to play with and almost no adult supervision, he turned to Rom, the houseboy.

One day he saw Rom steal two cans of sardines from the pantry in the kitchen. Rom could lose his job and his income if he were caught. Gary understood this and promised he would not tell his parents about Rom's theft if Rom would take him off of the compound.

Rom had an old bicycle and mounted a board across the handlebars where Gary could ride. On their first trip out of the compound, Gary was fascinated with the lush green forests and country roads he saw. Rom made sure that Gary was back before the canon sounded with his hands and face washed, just as his father had ordered.

On another trip, they found a cave. Rom warned Gary not to go in because it was dark and dangerous in there. The description of the cave only enticed Gary and he scrambled off the bike and began exploring before Rom could stop him. Just inside the cave he found bones of what he thought could have been a Filipino army officer who had died. Gary was frightened, but his sense of adventure overtook him. Knowing Rom was just behind him, Gary rushed forward to explore a passageway he saw at the back of the cave. Again Rom yelled at him to stop, but Gary ran ahead anyway. But when several large fuzzy animals pushed past him and one grabbed at his leg, Gary shrieked. Luckily Rom reached Gary in time and dragged him out. Rom told him the furry animals were rats that fed on dead bodies, since there were no graves for them.

Several weeks later, Eunice insisted that Oscar take the family on a weekend vacation. Military rules required that Ryland, since he was Officer Paulsen's aide, follow them. Even so, Gary hoped a vacation would mean that Eunice would smile and laugh again. But he wrote that it only meant more drinking.

Gary's father suggested they travel north of the compound

Did you know...

Many Filipinos are Christians who pray and celebrate Christmas from October through January. Morning mass takes place each morning for nine days before Christmas. On Christmas Eve, the worshipers attend a midnight mass. The day is spent visiting friends and relatives to wish them well and share banquets of food. They bring gifts, usually of food and money. Filipinos also decorate their houses with star-shaped lanterns of bright colored-paper and bamboo sticks. They string lights and candy on the Christmas Tree. By January 6 on the Feast of the Three Kings, the celebration is over. It is a special, meaningful holiday.

and visit the Sandiago Prison. He told Eunice that he had a friend who spent time there. When they arrived at the prison, Ryland and Gary followed Eunice and Oscar as they toured the facility. Paulsen wrote that he gathered more impressions he would use later in his books when he saw the tiny prison cells and metal instruments of torture. Actually, these were not so different from the cells and instruments he had seen in pictures of the inside of medieval prisons. There were racks that were used for stretching prisoners' arms and legs so far that the pain made them tell war secrets. Gary's father told him that prisoners were also starved, isolated and brainwashed by hearing lies about their own countrymen

But there was more. Oscar showed Gary and Eunice the mass-execution room where the Japanese burned American prisoners to death. There were no windows or bars in this room, no benches, or passageways through the heavy door. Gary remembers a brownish-yellow greasy film on the walls, which was actually residue from burned bodies. Gary never forgot this horror and kept a mental picture in his mind for weeks. Each time he remembered it, he was sick to his stomach.

Christmas 1947 was the Paulsens' first Christmas together in the Philippines. Gary was still seven years old, and as the holiday approached, Eunice tried to make it a special family event by attempting to carry on American holiday traditions. Eunice made a tree of bamboo and Gary and Rom helped make decorations from old tin cans and painted leaves. Eunice also baked Spam with cloves and cinnamon sticks.

Gary's father came home for lunch, but not with Christmas wishes or packages tied with ribbons. Instead, he had news. A typhoon was headed for the compound and would arrive by five o'clock that afternoon. He told his family to pack and be ready to go to a shelter in the city.

Right away Eunice gathered sheets and towels. She told Gary to help her. Marie and Rom packed nonperishable food that the family could eat without having to cook it. Eunice said they had to pack everything they might need, because their house and all of their belongings would probably be blown away.

Five o'clock arrived and Gary's father did not come. Shortly afterwards, they heard a jeep coming and Eunice started to relax. But Eunice mumbled harsh words of disappointment when she realized it was Sergeant Ryland and not her husband. Ryland said Officer Paulsen would join them at the shelter later.

The shelter was in the basement of a large office building in the city. There they found rows of cots lined up. Eunice claimed four cots—one for herself, one for her husband, one for Gary, and one for Maria. Rom would join his family at their home. Gary saw several children playing at one end of the shelter and with his mother's permission, went to join them. They played follow-the-leader, and skipping and hopping games.

Gary's father joined the family much later. The typhoon finally hit early the next morning. The sounds of thunderous rain and wind woke Gary. He slipped out of bed, climbed up on heating pipes, and looked out of the window. Torrential rains and gusty winds swept away everything in its path. Gary watched a Filipino crossing the parking lot by their building. The man staggered against the force of the wind, bouncing like a marionette. A tin roof broke loose from a hut nearby and took flight, hitting the man squarely in the neck. Next it swirled back and attacked him again, this time hitting him across his body. Several officers from the shelter quickly ran out to assist the man and dragged him out of the winds.

Later that morning, the wind died as the typhoon passed. It was time to return to the compound. Rom picked up Maria and, with a crew from his village, they rebuilt the houses in the compound, complete with mesh walls and wrapped rattan furniture. Lizards immediately took residence in the ceiling of the living room and black ants settled back in the faucets.

Life returned to its usual routine for Gary. Sergeant Ryland picked up Gary's father each day and his mother visited with the other wives in the compound. The drinking and abuse he suffered from his parents were something he dreaded, but grew to accept.

Each day Eunice and other servicemen's wives would play cards and chat. By five o'clock Officer Paulsen would come home, escorted by Ryland. Then Eunice and Oscar would begin drinking steadily until late in the night. By morning, it would start over.

Gary spent more and more time with Rom in his Filipino village. He learned to like Filipino dishes like rice and sardines. He learned some of the language and he often spent hours sitting against the wall being very quiet like the Filipino children did. The children learned to stay quiet for long periods of time so that when soldiers came through their village, they would think the Filipino shacks were empty. Gary also learned to stand on one leg for long periods of time, like the Filipino children did.

That spring the family went on a real vacation. They traveled to the Bagiou Mountains north of Manila. The Bagiou Mountain people were famous for their arts and

In the Philippines, Gary spend time with his family's "houseboy" Rom in his village and learned things from the other Filipino children, including the language and how to stay quiet for long periods of time—a habit picked up from wartime in order to fool soldiers into thinking that villages were deserted.

crafts. They set up little shops and craft stands to sell their goods to the tourists. When the family stopped to shop for local merchandise, Gary learned something else about his mother, a trait he values in himself.

Eunice was attracted to a work of art one of the mountain people had for sale, so she demanded that Officer Paulsen stop the jeep. She began by offering the shop owner two dollars for the picture that he had marked to sell for ten dollars. Eunice and the shop owner talked back and forth. Eunice got the picture for four dollars. She did this again with another work of art. Gary was so impressed with her talent for bargaining that he never forgot it. He would use this skill later when he was off on his own traveling with the circus and working in the fields as a migrant worker.

Gary also found a little dog when they visited the Bagiou Mountains. He named it Snowball because it had a coat of white fluffy fur. Snowball and Gary became very close and he often told Snowball things he would not tell anyone else. He had finally found a companion to take the place of Dog. Unfortunately, his time with Snowball would be short as well.

One day Gary and Snowball were walking by the fence in the compound when a truck, swerving to miss the pair, accidentally ran over Gary's dog. One of the servicemen jumped out of the truck. Gary was crying and the little dog was in great pain. The officer shot the little dog dead, putting it out of its misery. Although he was heartbroken, Gary understood what had happened and accepted it. The officer put his arm around Gary and told him he was very brave. Gary cried again, but there was no one the seven-year-old could turn to for comfort.

Christmas the next year, 1948, was another disaster. This time Eunice found a live tree and she, along with Rom and Gary, decorated it with the tops of coffee cans and colored paper. After this, Gary was left alone to play in his room as Eunice went out to drink and play bridge with the other women. He heard a jeep pull up and thought it was his father. Instead, when he walked out to the kitchen, he saw his mother and Ryland in an embrace. He piped up, "Does this mean I have to call him Uncle?"

His mother was so shocked and angry she slapped Gary across the face. But he stood his ground defiantly, even after she slapped him again. He went to his room but refused to cry, and thought that if he told his father, that he might have Ryland and maybe his mother killed. In the end, he didn't—because of the Christmas holiday. His mother came into the bedroom crying and apologized to Gary. Gary however would not accept her apology and again confronted her with her cheating on his father. She resumed drinking whiskey until Oscar came home.

When he did, Gary remembered that "it was as if none of it had happened." Then Officer Paulsen also started drinking. Gary remembers the big role drinking had in his life when he was young and lived with his parents. Several adults in his books were heavy drinkers and the main character, a teenager (that the reader readily understands is Gary), suffers from neglect and abuse. In fact, Paulsen's his book *The Island* is about a young boy who is taken from his home when his parents become so abusive that a social worker takes the boy away from his parents.

The abuse Gary suffered on that Christmas, 1948, however, was completely devastating. Gary and his father were admiring the tree when all of a sudden Eunice cried out that they should be decorating the tree on Christmas Eve. She pulled the decorations off and threw them to Gary and Oscar, demanding they put them back on the tree. Gary remembered that his mother laughed in a crazy way. Her voice was low-pitched and husky. Finally, they all gave up the artificial celebration and went to bed.

On Christmas Day, Eunice told Gary that they were "going home."

"But this is our home . . . " Gary said.

"No. It isn't," said his mother.

Gary could hardly believe that they could leave behind their life in the Phillipines. But six days later, the Paulsens were on a plane heading back to Minneapolis, and Gary was left to wonder if things were going to get any better back in America with the whole family together.

Once back from the Philippines, Gary would spend summers with relatives in northern Minnesota. He found the landscape to be a refreshing change of pace from Minneapolis, and this undoubtedly had an impact on his future decision to run the Iditarod.

4

Popcorn Days

GARY HOPED WITH all of his heart that things would be different when they returned to the United States. But, even at eight years old, Gary knew that when his parents were drinking, they would soon be fighting.

The trip home began with a military plane taking the family to a nearby island where they were picked up by a seaplane. Then they boarded a Pan Am Clipper for the long journey to the United States. Even though the trip would cover the same seven thousand miles they had traveled from San Francisco to Manila, their journey across the Pacific Ocean to the

United States was much quicker since the only stops they made were for refueling.

Once on board, crew members gave Gary soda, candy, and games. When Gary tired of snacks and games, he scooted over to the window seat and stared down at the vast ocean. His thoughts filled with the crash of the plane he and his mother had witnessed on their trip from San Francisco two years earlier. He remembered how his mother had helped with the passengers from the plane and the sight of the two little girls in his bunk, hugging Dog.

The trip back to the United States was smooth and uneventful, leaving Gary with time for thoughts of living in Minneapolis again. He remembered friends in his neighborhood and wondered if they were still there. He remembered his bedroom with pictures on the wall and the streetlight shining in his window. He also remembered hot dogs, hamburgers, French Fries, and peanut butter. But mostly, he hoped the return home would stop the fighting and drinking. But that was wishful thinking.

The family returned to the apartment where Gary and his mother Eunice lived when he was a baby. The fights between his parents continued. Many times they went on all day and late into the night. Often Gary was left on his own to wander the streets.

Gary was eleven when Eunice, in a drunken rage, captured her son under the kitchen table and threatened him with a knife. When she came to her senses, she realized she could not adequately care for Gary, so she sent him to northern Minnesota to live with his grand-mother. Gary spent the next seven summers living in Northern Minnesota with his mother's relatives. He loved his mother and would miss her, but he looked forward to summers away from the city when school was out. He was always glad to see his mother again in the fall, but the situation at home did not change.

Paulsen's book, *Popcorn Days and Buttermilk Nights*, recounts tales of one summer when he was fourteen. It was 1953 and Gary was visiting his Uncle David in Norstem, the small community in northern Minnesota, where Uncle David and his family lived. At first, the beauty of the trees and the charm of unpaved roads held his attention, and he was enchanted by the little lakes that seemed to cry out for summer swimmers.

Uncle David was a farmer and raised Holsteins and chickens. He was also a blacksmith, supporting his family of seven children and his wife, Emily. Gary, fresh from the city—where his life on the street was filled with gangs, drunks, and living on the edge of the law—found love and respect at his uncle's house. When his train arrived in Norstem, Uncle David took him to the forge where he hammered metal for farm tools and horseshoes. Before the afternoon was over, Gary had learned to crank the bellows to feed the coal fire. He helped his uncle hammer new shoes on the horses his neighbors brought to him, and he felt a sense of importance. Gary's face was soon covered with grime and black from the thick smoke. Only the whites of his eyes were a normal color. When Uncle David announced it was time to go home, Gary's muscles cried out with fatigue—but it was a good kind of tiredness. Gary had not felt so appreciated since he was six years old when he and his mother were close.

Uncle David slid into the seat of an old wagon drawn by two weary-looking farm horses. He whispered to the animals, patting each one on the flank with the reins, and motioned Gary to climb on the board seat beside him. The wagon bounced along hitting every rut and pothole on the road. Gary's bag slid back and forth across the cargo bed, but he was too tired to check on it. The two miles they traveled to the farm seemed like ten miles to Gary. But he perked up quickly when the wagon slowed and they rode onto the farm.

The farm appeared shabby to the city-bred Gary. He saw paint peeling from the sides of the house and chickens running loose. The greatest surprise was to see children washing at a horse trough in the front yard. The children's clothes were patched and tattered, but they did not seem to mind. Crowding together, they spilled as much water on the ground as they did on themselves.

The welcome that Gary felt when he met Uncle David at the train station was multiplied ten-fold when he met the rest of the family. There were seven kids, ranging in age from three to seven. Aunt Emily stepped out from the kitchen door, followed by the most marvelous odors of food Gary could imagine. He would never forget these

Did you know...

Forging, shaping metal by hand, is one of the oldest occupations known to man. The forger, or blacksmith, heats the metal in a furnace until it is red hot. He uses tongs to lift the hot metal from the forge and hammers it against an anvil, a heavy metal block, to get the shape he wants.

wonderful smells. Writing about this experience later, he recalled Emily smiling as she wiped her hands on her apron. "Dinner soon. Put your stuff upstairs, and come down and wash," she said.

In spite of the welcome, Gary felt like an outsider, even though Uncle David was his mother's brother. When Uncle David showed him upstairs where he would sleep in a room with the other children, Gary was amazed at the sight. The walls were rafters, not finished walls like he had in his bedroom at home. Here Gary would sleep in a bunk bed with people all around him. He tried to stow his bag under the bed that Uncle David said was his, but there was no room. Looking under the bed, Gary saw that it was made of rope and that there were no box springs. All of a sudden he felt sick to his stomach. He missed his room at home and he missed his parents, even with their drinking and fighting.

When Uncle David told him to come down and eat, he shook his head mumbling he was not hungry. Later that evening Uncle David came up, took the fourteen-year-old by the hand and led him back down to the kitchen where Emily had saved a plate of meat and potatoes for him. Uncle David and Emily joined him with a cup of coffee. Gradually, Gary felt the love of the family surround him.

The summer passed. Gary grew a couple of inches and gained weight. He had learned iron-forging, ridden a bull, and become a friend to his seven-year-old cousin, Tinker. When his uncle decided to make a circus for his children, Gary helped by bending the iron for the Ferris Wheel and the merry-go-round. Neighbors pitched in, sewing seats for the rides and setting up booths for popcorn and cotton candy.

Paulsen wrote that it seemed more of a fair than a circus. But he felt wonderful in that he had helped his uncle build a circus for his children.

In September, Gary went back to Minneapolis, and his mother and father were still fighting and drinking. Stephanie True Peters wrote in her biography of Gary Paulsen that Gary's father tried to raise chickens, but he failed and money got tighter and tighter. This did not help matters at home.

Gary was fifteen in May 1954, and again his parents shipped him off to relatives in northern Minnesota. He wrote about this summer in his book called *Tiltawhirl John*, which was published by Puffin Books in 1977. This time he lived with Uncle Ernest Peterson and his wife Florence on a wheat farm. Uncle Ernest treated Gary as his own son and even bequeathed eighty acres of wheat farm to him, showing Gary the will. Gary however was not sure he wanted to be a farmer and earn his living from the land. So one afternoon shortly after he had seen the will, Gary ran away to make his own way.

Having heard that a beet farm just outside of Jefferson, North Dakota was hiring workers for $12 an acre, he walked to the highway near his uncle's farm and hitch-hiked. The first leg of his trip was in the back of a truck carrying hogs—and he never forgot the smells and feel of hog waste. When Gary finally arrived at the beet farm, the owner, Karl Elsner, put him to work right away hoeing fields of beets. Gary thought the job would be easy and he would make a lot of money. But when Gary asked Elsner for his money, Elsner beat him and charged him for the beans and dried bread he had eaten and for the mat where he slept. Gary knew then that Elsner was taking advantage of him. He also knew that Elsner could

Gary ran away from a tyrannical beet farm owner and briefly joined a traveling carnival. He even learned how to operate the Tiltawhirl ride and earned $35 a week, but witnessing a violent knife fight between two of the carneys made him decide to go back to his uncle's wheat farm.

report him to the authorities as a runaway and he would be sent back to his uncle's farm. Gary and Elsner fought, and Elsner broke Gary's arm and bruised his back and legs. Gary crawled away, hiding in a ditch at the edge of the farm. He dragged himself to the highway away from the beet farm and never went back.

Gary was lucky when a truck stopped on the highway to pick him up. His rescuers were Wanda, T-John, and Billy—carnival folks. They nursed him back to health and offered him a job. Gary learned to run the Tiltawhirl, a ride with seats that turned as it went around, like a Ferris wheel. Wanda, the exotic dancer, and Billy, the pretend side-show freak, became family to Gary. He made $35 a week and he felt successful. At fifteen, Gary thought he had found his life's work. But several months later, Gary witnessed a knife fight between T-John and Tucker, another carney. The battle was bloody and Tucker was killed. Gary was shocked. Now he understood how dangerous the carney way of life could be. When the police arrived, Gary told them he was a runaway and they took him back to his Uncle's wheat farm. He determined there were worse careers than being a wheat farmer. His uncle understood him and welcomed him home.

Later that summer, Gary would find work with a friend in southern Minnesota. He worked for one dollar and five cents an hour at a Birdseye frozen vegetable factory in Waseca. He stayed with his friend in a town called Monkato that was over twenty miles from the job. It was at this time that Gary began his love affair with motorcycles. He had to walk or hitch-hike to work every day and he was usually late, so Gary's boss had a solution for him. He offered Gary an old Whizzer bike with flat tires and a missing spark plug for ten dollars. A Whizzer was a late 1930s motorbike which was originally sold as a kit for $54.95. The boss who sold it to Gary warned him that he would have to choke the engine repeatedly until the bike started. The bike had a personality of its own—it was by no means dependable and took constant care. But

Gary's first motorbike was the Whizzer, which was originally sold as a kit in the 1930s. Although it was tempermental and required constant maintenance, it instilled in Gary dreams of owning his own real motorcycle.

it didn't matter to Gary, as he was thrilled with the bike. Everyday he coasted down hill and choked the bike to get it started, and even started to make it to work on time— at least on most days. A seed was planted in Gary's mind, and he dreamed that one day, he'd have a real motorbike of his own.

Gary found a job setting pins at a bowling alley in 1954. His high school years would prove to be pivotal ones in his life, as he found a father figure in D.J., and discovered books thanks to a friendly librarian.

5

Turning Point

SEPTEMBER CAME AND fifteen-year-old Gary was back in Minneapolis and on the streets. Even though Gary still lived with his parents, he did not see them often. To get spending money, he got a job setting pins at a bowling alley and sold newspapers in bars. Gary did poorly in school and frequently played hooky.

He was also lonely most of the time. But one day companionship came in the form of Dirk, a large scraggy-haired dog with two glowing yellow eyes. Gary described him as an "Airdale crossed with hound crossed with alligator." Dirk made his entrance into Gary's life by protecting him against the street gangs who chased him and made his life miserable. One evening, one of the bowling leagues rolled a high score. To celebrate, they gave Gary and the other pit boys hamburgers and cokes. Gary planned to take his back to his basement retreat, so instead of leaving through the front door, he slipped out a second floor window and climbed down a ladder. As he reached the bottom, he heard an angry snarl. Fortunately, Gary was wise to the ways of strays and knew the dog was hungry. Gary was hungry too, but he knew he could distract the animal by throwing him food. So, Gary tossed him half his sandwich and ran.

Maybe, Gary thought, he could run fast enough to escape the bullies and get home safely. But the gang was waiting for him around the corner. Although he was hit and beaten, Gary fought back, but finally fell to the ground and curled up. But it was Dirk who fought them off by biting one of the gang members and tearing off part of his jeans. So when he growled for the rest of the hamburger, Gary willingly rewarded him. After that Dirk followed Gary wherever he went. He even shared Gary's retreat by the furnace in the basement of his apartment. Gary gave his friend and protector some of his peanut butter and jelly crackers.

One evening Gary spotted new skis propped up against the wall in a garage. There was no one around so Gary thought he could break in, steal the skis and sell them. He didn't get away with the crime. In *Pilgrimage on a Steel Ride*, Paulsen explains how D.J., a cop, interrupted him. D.J. forced Gary's arm behind his back and asked "What were you doing?"

"I was going to break into the garage."

"For what?"

"I need a place to stay. My folks are drunks and . . . "

He pushed my arm up again. "I know your old man. He's a
　　drunk but he ain't that mean. Why were you breaking in?"

"To take a pair of skis."

"To *steal* a pair of skis."

"Yes."

D.J. put him in the patrol car and headed out of town.
After six or seven miles, he made Gary get out and walk
in front of the patrol car in the freezing weather. D.J. told
him to think about what he had planned to do and how
badly he would be treated if he tried it again. He said if
Gary said he was sorry and promised not to steal again,
he could ride in the car—otherwise, he would have to
walk back to town. But Gary was stubborn and pulled his
light jacket close against his body with his hands jammed
in the pockets. D.J. followed him in the car. Gary's hands
and feet were so cold they were numb—but in spite of the
freezing weather, Gary was determined to not say he was
sorry. Consequently, he walked the whole way. It took
him two hours.

Gary finally got in the patrol car with D.J. when they
arrived in town. Instead of taking Gary to the police
station, D.J. surprised him by taking him to Harry's, an
all-night diner. Gary was starved and stared at a greasy
hamburger and fries on the plate of a man sitting at
the counter.

D.J. seemed to know everyone in the diner. He told the
waitress that Gary was a growing boy and needed a
healthy meal. She gave him a plate of mashed potatoes,
meat loaf, and canned green beans—but Gary was so

hungry and cold that anything would have tasted wonderful. D.J. paid for the meal, and over the next two years Gary met with D.J. at Harry's almost every evening after his shift at the bowling alley. But after that first free meal, D.J. made Gary pay seventy-cents for his meal and leave a ten-cent tip.

One cold January evening, Gary was walking slowly along the street, waiting for D.J. to pick him up. With his hands in his pockets and his jacket pulled tightly against him, he longed for some place to get out of the cold. The lights in the library building across the street looked inviting. Even though it was merely the cold that drove Gary to cross the street and slip into the building, it turned out to be a turning point in his life.

Gary was used to people looking at him suspiciously, so he was surprised when the librarian greeted him with a smile on her face. She asked him if he would like help choosing a book. Gary dropped his head and mumbled to himself. School at that time was a chore to Gary, if he attended at all—so the idea of reading, let alone choosing a book, wasn't an appealing one. Nevertheless, when the librarian held out a thin volume and said she thought he might like it, he took the book from her. He opened the book and began to read slowly. Then the librarian helped him get a library card and check the book out. She also showed him how to use the card catalog and find other books on subjects that interested him.

Eventually the librarian became Gary's friend and going to the library became a habit. Gary would books on travel, entertainment, and survival stories, and the librarian would discuss some of the stories with him. Gradually, he worked his way into classics like *Moby Dick* and *Tom Sawyer*, and soon fell in love with books.

Moby Dick *by Herman Melville was one of the first books that Gary
checked out from the library. Reading these books made an impact on
his own writing, and he would spend more and more time reading them
in his basement instead of selling newspapers in bars.*

He continued setting pins at the bowling alley, but he gave up going to bars to sell newspapers so he could spend the time reading. Gary would sneak a box of his favorite crackers and munch away with Dirk at his side as he sat in the old chair in the basement of his apartment building. He wrote in *Pilgrimage on a Steel Ride* that his love of reading good books helped him in his writing, as he began to see different styles of writing and how characters are developed.

At about 10:30 at night when the bowling leagues were over, Gary would go down to meet D.J. Dirk would trail after him and Gary always saved a scrap of his dinner for the dog. He said that D.J. was like a father to him, talking to him about his experiences as a cop and in Vietnam. Gary had given up hanging around on the streets at night. His chair in the basement was his sanctuary, a place away from the bars, and away from the fights and drunken behavior of his parents.

Gary was nineteen when he graduated from Thief River Falls High School High school in 1957 with a D-minus average. After graduation, Gary enlisted in the army, since there seemed nothing else for him to do. He was stationed in Fort Bliss in El Paso, Texas. One day, about a year later Paulsen received a letter from a friend of D.J.'s. The letter said a fifteen-year-old who had stolen his father's car for a joyride killed D.J. The kid had a high-powered rifle and when D.J. approached him, the kid shot him.

Paulsen remembers that when he read this letter, he was so angry and went crazy. He tried to get leave so he could go back and kill the kid. But twenty-year-old Paulsen was married by then and had a child of his own. He knew what would happen to his wife and child if he landed in

An older photo of Fort Bliss where Gary was stationed after high school. In these three years, Paulsen felt like he really grew into a man, and he learned to handle jeeps, tanks, and missiles at Fort Bliss.

prison, so he did not go after D.J.'s killer. Paulsen spent three years in the army and he said he grew up in those years. He learned to handle jeeps, tanks, and missiles.

After the army, Paulsen took jobs ranging from cleaning septic tanks to repairing Harley-Davidson bikes. He got divorced, started drinking, and took a job in the aerospace industry where he spent his time behind a computer. After a while Paulsen decided there must be a better way to earn a living than sitting behind a computer reviewing other people's writing. He knew in his heart he could be a writer, so he made up a false resume. He knew this was wrong, but he thought if he got a job as a writer, he would become one. No one was really fooled, but finally a men's magazine that was desperate for writers took a chance on him. Even though his boss recognized that his resume was made up, he convinced his boss that he was eager and intelligent. He was lucky not to be fired.

Every night Paulsen wrote something. His writing improved as he noticed more details about people, which made his own characters ring true. He married again. And after 11 months he sold his first article.

Soon other magazines recognized his talent and he was asked to speak at writers' conferences. In his auto-biography, *Pilgrimage on a Steel Ride*, he tells how he gave up his job at the magazine to pursue writing as a craft and as a career. His next move was to an artist colony in New Mexico where he thought he could become wealthy selling articles and books. Instead he became an alcoholic.

Gary bought an old Chevy Chevette. After fixing up a bunk on the fold-down seat in the back, he toured writing conferences to learn more about his craft and to make money as a speaker. At the same time he began selling his work to better magazines and began to write books. His first book, *Special War*, that was about life with his alcoholic father, came out in 1966. Over the next eleven years he published nearly forty books and several articles and short stories. In *Pilgrimage on a Steel Ride* he describes his audience at writing conferences. He said many of them wanted to "Have Written"—that is, these conference-goers wanted the thrill of publication without the hard work and the pain of rejection. He used the same speech over and over again until it became meaningless to him. He continued to drink and his debts piled up. His visits home became irregular. He fought with his second wife and they divorced.

However, throughout his ups and downs as a writer and his failed marriages, Paulsen's love of motorcycles stayed with him. One day he stopped by a bike shop where two bikes were parked in front. One was a Red Harley Dasher bike and the other was a Softtail. Right away dreams of freedom from all of his worries filled his mind. He envisioned riding the road, the wind against him, and the hum of the motor beneath him. He said the salesman looked at him with "pity in his eyes" when Paulsen confessed he could not afford a Harley at that time. It would be over twenty years before he realized his dream.

One day, with a check for $200 in his hand, he stood in the line at the bank to make his deposit. Spotting a policeman, he was afraid he would be apprehended since he was so much in debt. Fate stepped in when he took a chance and slipped his check to a young woman standing behind him in line. He whispered to her to deposit his check for him and she did. Her name was Ruth and like Paulsen, she had a love of art, being an artist herself. Several months after their meeting at the bank, Ruth became Gary's third wife.

In 1977, Paulsen wrote *Winterkill*, a book about characters he had known and about alcoholism. He was sued when some people he had known recognized themselves in his book. Even though he eventually won the law case, lawyers and court fees wiped out his savings.

Poverty and Paulsen's love of animals and the cold weather drew Ruth and him back to Minnesota where they settled on a small farm with their young son, Jim. Paulsen often mentions the early years of his marriage to Ruth. He was writing full time, but not making enough money to support the family. He said they lived in a lean-to shack with an outhouse. He took temporary construction and maintenance jobs. Paulsen's books were selling, but money from his writing was still not enough to support his family. His publishers arranged book signings for him. These were usually scheduled in libraries, books stores, and sometimes hotels. For a signing, the author sits at a table with a stack of his books by his side. Sometimes people buy the books and then ask for the author's autograph.

Following one such visit in Chicago, Paulsen began to have chest pains. When he consulted his doctor, he found he had a serious heart condition. The doctor's advice

Did you know...

Interest in beaver fur for wealthy lady's hats began in late 1700's in Europe and spread to Canada. The pelts of fur-bearing animals like beaver, fox, and mink were sought along the Great Lakes. In 1784 Grand Portage on the Pigeon River in Michigan became "Great Carrying Place" for fur trading. The company hired backwoods hunters from Michigan and Minnesota to provide them with furs.

following his examination was that Paulsen must give up drinking and high-fat foods. At first these changes were hard for Paulsen to accept, but finally he agreed to them. That wasn't the only thing to change drastically in Paulsen's life. Though these were hard times, it was during this period that his love of dogs would take him on an adventure unlike any he'd ever known.

In 1977, Paulsen's expanding trap-setting business eventually led him to working with a team of dogs, planting the seeds of future visions of dogracing glory.

6

The Musher and His Dogs

DOGS HAD ALWAYS been important as companions and protectors to Paulsen. He never forgot his toy dog, Dog, that he had when he and his mother traveled to the Philippines to meet his father. And he would never forget Snowball, who meant so much to him when he lived in the Philippines. But when he and Ruth moved to northern Minnesota and he became a trapper, dogs became his livelihood.

Paulsen wrote, "I am—I say this with some pride and not a little wonder—a 'dog person' . . . They are wonderful and, I think, mandatory for decent human life."

With his new wife, Ruth, and their young son, they lived in a shack in the northern woods. They also had a kennel for Rex, a mixed collie that became Gary's next canine companion. Paulsen cultivated a farm around the lean-to and the family lived on the vegetables and chickens they raised. Rex lived on table scraps. Paulsen also hunted small animals like squirrel and beaver, and an occasional deer. Since his time was flexible, Paulsen also volunteered for the fire and rescue service.

Eventually, Paulsen added cows and a barn. Rex was now not only a companion to his master but also a guard for the livestock. Every morning he herded the cows to the field, checked on the animals in the barn and looked after the chickens. One night Rex caught a skunk trying to get at the chickens and he killed it. Paulsen recalled that saving the chickens was worth the smell that wafted through everywhere.

A Great Dane was the next dog to join the Paulsen family. When Caesar arrived, he took over everything in the house. Great Danes are known for their loyalty and Caesar missed his previous owner. Through patience and love, Paulsen and his family earned his affection. Rex also welcomed Caesar. Each dog had his own territory—Rex took care of the farm, and Caesar stayed in the house.

Even though Caesar was even-tempered, he was enormous. When Caesar stood on his hind legs, he was almost as tall as Paulsen. He was not fat either, but all muscle and weighing at least 150 pounds. Why would a family in a tiny lean-to farmhouse choose an animal like that? It was Paulsen's love of animals, especially dogs. He could not resist any animal needing a home. One day he responded to a sign advertising a loving Great

Dane who needed a home. Paulsen remembers how Caesar first made his entrance: "He sat for a moment, staring at me, then out the window; then he climbed on the couch, knocking over the coffee table, two end tables and a lamp . . . My wife looked around at the wreckage—when he'd jumped down he put his weight on the back of the couch and tipped it over—and sighed." However, Caesar proved he could do more for the Paulsens than destroy their furniture. He became a valuable member of Gary's son's baseball team, even "playing" left field. If a fly ball landed near Caesar, he carried it back to the pitcher. The kids loved the big dog and he loved the kids, especially when they fed him hot dogs.

In 1977, Paulsen began setting out beaver traps to collect furs to sell to the State of Minnesota. But it was only when a friend gave him four sled dogs that he could set enough traps to increase his income. The dogs' names were Storm, Yogi, Obeah, and Columbia. At the same time he received Cookie from another friend. She followed directions well and became his first sled dog leader. It was with these dogs that Paulsen began to learn how to handle dogs as a team.

Paulsen credits Cookie with saving him when he was training. Her story is told in *My Life in Dog Years* and repeated in different forms in *Woodsong* and *Dogsong*. He was racing across the snow and ice, looking for a way back home. He signaled the dogs to take a trail that led across a waterway covered with thin ice. Beavers lived beneath the ice and had scraped the underside thin in their attempt to get food. When the dogs hesitated to cross, Paulsen threw the rope that was attached to the sled across the ice and got out of the sled. He planned to grab Cookie by the cuff and force the team across.

A beaver trap being set. With his dogsled team, Paulsen could set more traps farther apart than he ever could before. After catching the beavers, he would sell their furs to the State of Minnesota.

Not surprisingly, Paulsen fell through the ice and into the freezing water. His parka and heavy gear acted like an anchor. He would have drowned if it weren't for Cookie pulling the team around and allowing Paulsen to grab the sled.

Paulsen wrote that he made many mistakes when he was training the dogs. Most of these occurred because he did not understand that sled dogs require special handling, long hours of training, and special diets. He learned these things as he trained the dogs and consulted with other sled dog owners.

Sled dogs are primarily working dogs. The American Kennel Association recommends that by the time they are 8 or 9 months old, they should be fed an adult diet, one that is high in meat and meat products, as cereal-based dog foods can tear at their digestive systems, which Paulsen found this out firsthand. On one of his practice runs, Paulsen noticed that Storm was bleeding from his rear end. He thought the dog was sick and tried to get him to lie down in the bed of the sled. Storm would have no part of resting. He leaped out of the sled and ran with the other dogs. Paulsen tried tying him beside the other dogs so he could run with them. He ran, but he was not pulling his share.

Finally, Paulsen let him run loose. Again he ran beside the others, but was not on the tug line, a rope that connects the dog's harness to the main rope of the sled and holds the dogs apart from one another as they run. Paulsen was afraid Storm would leap on the other dogs and tangle their leads. So he tied him back where he belonged. Paulsen was the one worried, not Storm. When he added more meat to the dog's diet, there was no more bleeding.

Columbia, another one of Paulsen's dogs, taught him about a dog's sense of humor. When the dogs returned from a run, each was chained to its house. The chains were long enough to give individual dogs their stretch room, but not long enough to allow it to reach the next dog. The dogs engaged in what Paulsen calls "Bone Wars." Each dog received a large beef bone to nibble on and play with.

Some of the dogs stood and waved their bones as if they were bragging about them.

But not Columbia. After eating all but one choice morsel from his bone, he dropped it just at the end of his chain, not quite close enough for his neighbor dog, Olah, to reach. Then he flopped down to watch. Olah saw the bone, clawed the ground and reached out with his front paws, then turned and tried to reach the prize with his hind paws. Paulsen swore that Columbia laughed as he watched Olah's frustration.

Paulsen learned that huskies are talkers, not barkers. They say, "woo-woo-woo" to those around them. Sled dogs do not bark excitedly when they begin a run— instead, they give one another messages with their eyes and perhaps mumble the "woo-woo-woo" sound. Once the run is started the only sounds are the runners of the sled moving along the trail.

Paulsen was also surprised to learn that his dogs actually sang. They sang a happy song when the moon was full and they were well fed. They also had a rain song and one about their fear of fire. Cookie, who was with Paulsen for fourteen years (from 1979 until her death in 1993), had five litters over her lifetime, and many of her offspring became Paulsen's most dependable sled dogs. Paulsen wrote how delighted he was when Cookie's puppies sang, each in his own high-pitched voice, little yips included. Each dog that joined Paulsen's team taught him valuable lessons that he would need when he actually ran the Iditarod.

The next four dogs were Duberry, Typhon, Devil, and Ortho. They came to him from Canada and were of mixed breed. They had been trained as sled dogs for four years, since they were pups. Paulsen discovered that some dogs on his team were "problem dogs" and each posed its own challenges. Some were too young, liked to fight too much, or spent too much time checking back to see what the sled driver was doing.

Duberry was the lead dog on one of his runs. She was small and quick. When a heavy snowstorm arrived, the wind knocked Paulsen off the sled and Duberry simply disappeared. He called and called for her. The next minute he slid down a mountain. He was deaf to everything except the screaming of the wind. His first concern was for the dogs. He continually called Duberry's name and he kept slipping. Fortunately the hook on his sled

Did you know...

Huskys are working dogs developed in the eastern Siberian Arctic. Throughout the last century they have mated with wolves and other sled dogs. Most have wolf colorings, dark brown or black backs and white fur on their faces and chests.

Training begins when the dogs are four months old. They must pull together as a team, handle long hours, and withstand temperatures of thirty degrees below freezing.

With the invention of sledmobiles, dependable trains, and improved plane service, sled dog running is no longer vital for transportation and has in recent years become an athletic competition. The best-known sled dog race is the Iditarod.

caught on a rock. He pulled himself onto a ledge and felt fairly safe. But where were the dogs and what had happened to the sled?

All of his food and camping equipment were no where to be seen. Then a miracle occurred. A shape, really a shadow, wobbling in the snow appeared. Grabbing at it, Paulsen's hand closed over the handlebar of the sled, with Duberry in the lead and the dogs still tied to it. One by one he pulled the sled and the dogs into his shelter. With her tug line hooked to the gang line, Duberry worked with Paulsen to pull all of the dogs into the shelter. He fed them, unzipped his sled bag, and drawing the dogs close around him settled in to wait for the storm to break. Paulsen wrote that when the dogs began to fight among themselves, he growled at them. Without the dogs, without Duberry pulling the team around, Paulsen would not have survived.

After this experience, Paulsen bought four more dogs from a Canadian trapper to add to his team. Their names were Typhon, Devil, Columbia, and Ortho. Paulsen and his wife borrowed an old pickup with a camper shell to pick them up. On the way, they went to a local pet store to buy plastic dog kennels to carry the dogs back in. Devil and Typhon immediately shredded their kennels. Ortho was a little slower, but soon his kennel, too, was nothing but a pile of scraps. Then the dogs started on the sides of camper, growling and tearing at the walls with their sharp teeth.

When Devil poked his head out the side of the camper, snarling with his teeth bared, Paulsen knew that he had to do something. Ruth suggested he ride in the back with the dogs and try to calm them down. They had two hundred miles to go.

The dogs stared at him when he slid into the back. His wife called, "They *like* you—it's going to be just fine . . . " With that, Ruth shifted the pickup into gear and they bounced down the road. Loving animals as he did, Paulsen tried to talk to Ortho and Devil, even reaching out to pet them. He learned very quickly that sled dogs do not want to be touched. All they want to do is run.

This was Paulsen's first attempt to put a team together to run the Iditarod. In *Woodsong*, he wrote that the Iditarod is not a human race, but a dog race. When Paulsen first hitched the dogs up to a sled for a trial run, the dogs disapproved and tossed him over. Next he tried hitching them to an old bicycle. The dogs chose their own way and dragged him for miles.

After that he tied an old English Ford sedan to the gang line behind the dogs. Taking off the doors and moving the seat back, his new sled was like a carriage, heavy enough so the dogs knew they were pulling something and comfortable enough for him. Paulsen stretched out comfortably, but this did not last very long. The dogs took off through the woods and over every rocky terrain they could find. Paulsen was worn out.

His next approach was to live with the dogs. He actually curled up on top of Cookie's house with his bedroll. This went on for several days. Ruth was very patient, even bringing him bowls of hot soup. By this time everyone in the town of Bemidji, Minnesota was pulling for Paulsen. The people of the town gave gifts of tires, gear for the dogs, dog food and human food. But Paulsen still did not have enough money until Richard Jackson, then editor-in-chief at Bradbury Press, stepped in with the funds Paulsen would need. In exchange, Paulsen promised Jackson a book on his experience running the Iditarod.

A close-up view of a driver on his dog sled. Besides learning how to ride the dogsled, Paulsen bonded with his dogs and even slept with them during the training for the Iditarod.

After three years of training and months of practice in Alaska before the race, Paulsen and his dogs were ready. He had reached an understanding of what was really involved in riding a sled:

> Riding was more a matter of fitting into the sled than trying to control it. With his knees relaxed and his hips loose he could shift his weight only slightly and the sled turned with him. It became almost an extension of his body, just as he was becoming almost an extension of the dogs.

Paulsen's first race in 1983 was successful; he made it to the finish line in Nome, Alaska. The following year he tried again, but this time he lost the dogs when they slid down an icy mountain, and Paulsen had to drop out of the race. Fortunately a rescue helicopter spotted them and airlifted them to safety. Despite the setback, Paulsen's memories of the Iditarod provided plenty of inspiration for stories about the dogs, the dangers, the dreams, and the successes.

It is not surprising that Gary's next trip was back to Alaska, but this time it would not be on a dogsled—but on a Harley-Davidson.

Paulsen and his wife Ruth settled in New Mexico in 1993, finally leaving the winters of Minnesota behind. But his writing still reflected adventurous lifestyles such as sailing and even historical fiction.

7

Life in New Mexico

IN 1993, PAULSEN sold his farm in Northern Minnesota and moved to a ranch in New Mexico. His medical doctor prescribed rest, but rest was difficult for the fifty-four-year-old adventurer. And as a writer, he continued to thrive on adventures by writing stories about them.

His companion and friend at this time was a border collie named Josh. Paulsen dubbed him "The Smartest Dog in the World." Paulsen wrote of him, "He is . . . real. No, more than that, he is a person."

Paulsen had great fun with Josh. He would dress him in a baseball cap and sunglasses. When he told Josh how cool he looked,

Josh would put his right front paw on the ledge of the window and nod in agreement. Josh did the same thing when Paulsen ordered a sandwich at a drive-through window. Josh did other things, too. He hurried to the phone every time it rang and he maneuvered Paulsen's mare away from the other horses when Paulsen wanted to go for a ride.

Being home also gave Paulsen time to spend with his wife Ruth. Ruth was an artist and became Paulsen's illustrator for *Puppies, Dogs and Blue Northers* and *My Life in Dog Years*.

He also went sailing. Paulsen fell in love with boats when he and his mother had boarded the carrier boat in 1945 to visit his father in the Philippines. He bought his first boat in 1965, three years after he left the service. Later in life, he fixed up an old sailboat, which he named *Felicity*, so he and Ruth could take ocean voyages from Mexico and the Sea of Cortez, also called the Gulf of California.

Later he purchased a sailboat with twin hulls called a catamaran. He called this boat *Ariel*, and with it he was able to take longer trips, even going across the Pacific and back home to Mexico. He sailed for many years and enjoys it today. He liked to sail from Southern California to the South Pacific to the coast of Alaska. From there he would go to Hawaii and back to Mexico.

Storms that Paulsen experienced while sailing the *Felicity* and on his trip to the Philippines gave Paulsen ideas for new stories about the sea. In the *Voyage of the Frog*, Paulsen tells the story of 14-year-old David Alspeth who is given a sailboat by his Uncle Owen. David's adventures recall Paulsen's traumatic experiences when Paulsen bought his own first boat, a Schock 22, which was three years old. He did not know how to sail or maneuver the boat and lost control. Only by trial and error did he find his way back to the dock.

In 1995, he published *Danger on Midnight River*, a story

about three boys en route to a summer camp when the driver of the camp van loses his way. The driver drowns when the van slips into the river, and the boys are lost in the woods. Brandon, the main character, uses the skills he learned in spending summers with his uncle in the Rocky Mountains to save the boys and finally reach safety. Many of Paulsen's sea adventures went into his writing of *Caught by the Sea, My Life on Boats* published in October 2001.

Paulsen's famous book *Hatchet*, which was a Newbery Honor Book, was written while he was training for his first Iditarod in 1983. But two of his best-selling sequels to *Hatchet* were written after he and Ruth moved to their ranch in New Mexico—*Brian's Winter* and *Brian's Return*.

Guts is Paulsen's book about the story behind *Hatchet* and the Brian Books. Here he describes his own adventures living and surviving the woods of North Dakota and Minnesota. Paulsen tells how he forced himself to have every experience Brian had, including eating eyeballs and guts of animals.

Paulsen also branched out in other directions with his writing. He wrote about the slavery in the early nineteenth century in *Sarney* and *Nightjohn*. In these books, learning to read is the symbol of hope, just as reading became Paulsen's own salvation when he was in his teens.

He also wrote stories of the Civil War years. *Soldier's Heart* is a powerful story about a fifteen-year-old Charles who signs up with the First Minnesota Volunteers. Paulsen was always interested in history, and he had spent time in the service himself. He also saw the devastation of war when he was very young during his time in the Phillipines. Charley ends up fighting at Bull Run and Gettysburg. The horror of the war, the killing of his companions, and his own suffering age Charley, and when he returns home four years later at the age of nineteen, he is no longer a boy.

In 1996, Paulsen finally realized his dream of owning a Harley by purchasing a Heritage Softail motorcycle like the one shown here. Given his age and his history of heart disease, he felt that his biological clock was running out and that he had to buy a motorcycle now before it was too late.

Two Wheels at Last

PAULSEN WAS THIRTY-EIGHT years old in 1977 when he had first stopped to admire a Red Harley Dasher and a Softail in front of a bike shop. Now he was fifty-seven and the year was 1996. Through diet and exercise, his heart disease was gone, at least when he was quiet. He felt a tremendous urgency to be on the go again. He wrote:

> I could not stop it, could never stop it and I knew it then, knew I had to leave, to get moving again, to seek, to continue the run for the rest of my life and that if I stopped, even for a moment, "it" would catch up with me—what "it" was— and I would stop. Stop forever.

"It" may have been his own mortality, or at the very least, a sense of complacency and lack of adventure, which he wanted to avoid at all costs. The next adventure in his life would take the form of his own motorcycle.

He had several bikes through his growing up years following his first bike, the Whizzer. He had an English bike, "a Triumph . . . so beautiful it was almost a shame to ride it. Next came other bikes with brakes and assorted options like two and three gears, side mirrors, and CD players. Many of these were impractical and unreliable.

As Gary enjoyed greater success in his writing career, his dreams of owning the Harley-Davidson became more vivid. One day he stopped in front of a shop with "Harley-Davidson" painted in bold letters across the front window. He told the salesman he wanted to purchase one.

The salesman answered, "You've come to the right place." Paulsen admired two bikes in particular—a Fat Boy, red and glistening, and a Softail Custom, painted turquoise-green. As he pointed to each one in turn, the sales man gave him the bad news—that the bikes were sold. Paulsen asked about several other bikes that were on display, and again, the salesman told him they were sold. Finally the salesman told Paulsen he could order a bike.

"How long," Paulsen asked, "How long will it take to get the bike?"

The salesman answered, "We can fax that (the order) so that won't take any time . . . say just at three years."

Paulsen was stunned. He explained that he was already fifty-six years old and had heart disease.

"There is at least a chance I won't be around for three more years," he said.

The salesman answered in a matter-of-fact tone, "Then you'll want a used bike."

Leading Paulsen into the back, he showed him a blue-and-chrome Heritage Softail with spiked wheels, a windshield and wide front end fog lights. Even as he pointed to it, Paulsen got excited. The salesman said, "But like I said, I'm sure it's sold."

Upon Paulsen's urging, the salesman investigated the ticket. "No," the salesman said, "The guy bought it and his old lady made him bring it back." Without thinking twice, Paulsen said, "I'll buy it."

The bike alone cost over $19,000 dollars. He also bought a helmet, jacket, and goggles. Three hours passed as the salesman explained the features and checked his credit. Finally, Paulsen was able to sit on the bike and put the key in the ignition. He said he felt "strange but in some way whole."

That night he dreamed about the trip he would take. He wanted to ride back to Alaska, to travel across the state from Anchorage to Nome, following the trail he took in March 1983 in his first Iditarod race. He studied maps of the United States and decided his trip would be over ten thousand miles round trip.

Paulsen practiced riding his bike. Each day he increased the distance and built up his own endurance. He got to know the bike and he got to know himself as a biker. Having met a newly retired sergeant from the air force at the Harley dealer, he found a comrade for his trip. The sergeant's name was Larry and the two became friends immediately.

Many Harley riders like the ones shown here enjoy traveling great distances on their bikes. Paulsen, along with a companion, did just that, and in their journey they also retraced the Iditarod trail.

They agreed to go together and planned their route. It would go from his home in New Mexico through Sante Fe across Texas up through Kansas, Colorado, into Nebraska, South Dakota, over to Minnesota, and from there across Canada into Alaska, arriving in Anchorage to begin following the Iditarod trail. They planned to ride 500 miles a day and sleep in cheap motels at night. The trip would take about three weeks.

Paulsen said that traveling north, they received more and more comments about the Harley. People wondered why two middle-aged men would be chasing across the north and following the route of the Iditarod on motorcycles. He also ran into problems like groups of motor homes that clogged the roadways and snowmobile routes. The tires on the Harley did not respond the way runners of sleds had.

Paulsen also ran into a gull in Canada near Lake

Did you know...

A Harley-Davidson dealer in Tacoma Washington named a group of owner-enthusiasts HOG. The initials stand for Harley Owners Group. The group has special activities including day trips and overnight weekend trips. They also have vacation suggestions, dances, concerts, holiday parties and barbecues for their members. Members laughingly call themselves HOGs.

Superior. He had been riding along at eighty miles an hour when he spotted the bird on the side of the road pecking at a dead animal. He slowed his speed to seventy miles an hour. At that moment the gull flew toward Paulsen, and they collided. He remembers that "I hit the gull. Or we hit together." The gull struck the bike just below the headlight, shaking the bike, and catching Paulsen in the stomach. The strength of the blow could have knocked him off the bike and killed him, but luckily he survived and was able to continue on his journey.

Through all of his adventure stories, Paulsen reminds the reader of the beauty of nature and the special relationship he feels to the land and animals. He quoted a chant from an ancient Navaho prayer that describes this love.

Above me there is beauty,
Below me there is beauty,
To my left there is beauty,
To my front there is beauty,
To my rear there is beauty,
There is beauty all around.

When Paulsen crossed the North Dakota-Montana border early one morning, he followed George Custer's trail in the 1876 campaign to round up the Sioux and Cheyenne Indians and bring them onto reservations. And he saw the house where Custer and his wife Libby had lived. Following Custer's course across the Montana prairie and back up to the Little Bighorn gave him an appreciation of Custer's Last Stand in the Sioux Wars.

When Paulsen arrived home, three weeks later, he was content to sit behind his laptop with Josh by his side, ready to tell his life stories through adventure and survival stories.

1939 Gary Paulsen is born to Oscar and Eunice Paulsen on May 17, 1939 in Minneapolis, Minnesota

Oscar Paulsen leaves to become career military officer

1944 Gary and his mother move to Chicago

1945 Gary and his mother travel to the Philippines to be with Gary's father

1948 The Paulsens return to United States and live in Minnesota

1957 Graduates from Thief River Falls High School

1958 Enlists in the army and is stationed in Fort Bliss, in El Paso, Texas

1962 Discharged from the army and works for an aerospace company in California

1965 Leaves the aerospace company to work for a men's magazine as an editor

1966 *The Special War*

Begins touring writer's conferences

1967 Moves to Taos, New Mexico where he meets his future wife, Ruth Wright, an artist

1971 Marries Ruth

Son Jim is born

1977 *Winterkill*

Sued by people who recognize themselves in *Winterkill*

1979 Wins *Winterkill* court case

Paulsens move to Minnesota where he begins trapping beavers for their furs

1980 A friend gives Gary his first dog team and sled

1981 Gives up trapping and begins training for the Iditarod

1982 Richard Jackson, then editor-in-chief at Bradbury Press, gives Gary the funds needed to enter the Iditarod

1983 Runs his first Iditarod, making it from Anchorage to Nome

1984 Runs the Iditarod again, but drops out of race after his dogs slip down an ice mountain

1986 *Dogsong*

Receives Newbery Honor Award for *Dogsong*

1988 *Hatchet*

Receives a second Newbery Honor Award, this time for *Hatchet*

1990 Following a book signing in Chicago, is diagnosed with
a heart ailment and must give up running dogs
Winter Room
Receives his third Newbery Honor Award for *Winter Room*

1991 Paulsens move back to New Mexico

1995 Buys a Harvey-Davidson; he and a friend retrace his steps to
Alaska and the Iditarod

1996 Buys a catamarand and outfits it to sail across the Pacific Ocean

HATCHET

Thirteen-year-old Brian Robeson leaves the city in a small plane to visit his father. Suddenly the pilot has a heart attack and the plane crashes. Brian must find his way to survive alone. A hatchet that his mother had given him is his only tool and his only weapon.

THE RIVER

Brian Robeson returns to the Canadian Wilderness with a psychologist Derek Holtzer. Derek plans to study how Brian survived the first time in *Hatchet*. Derek is struck by lightening and Brian builds a raft to carry him 100 miles to the nearest trading post.

BRIAN'S RETURN

Based on the premise that he was not rescued at the end of *Hatchet*, Brian tangles with the winter ice and snow in the Canadian Mountains. He makes a bow and arrow and shoots a bear as well as smaller animals for food. Kept from hunting by the deep snow, Brian observes how the rabbits use their forelegs as snowshoes to move about, so he uses bear hide and makes rope to fashion snowshoes for his survival.

BRIAN'S WINTER

This fourth and last book of the Brian story shows him with all the equipment he needs for survival in the Canadian Mountains. When his summer is past and it is time to return home, Brian drops his gear and walks off to live with nature on his own. He determines he will never be happy living in civilized society.

DOGSONG

Fourteen-year-old Russel Susskit leaves his own home and stays with Oogruk, an aged Eskimo who hasn't kept up with changes in social customs and has no idea how old he is. Russel learns Oogruk's songs of dogsledding and becomes one with the dogs. Russel saves a young pregnant woman, finds a bear, and kills it to have meat for the young woman. He leaves her for three days as he follows a snowmobile track to the nearest village. She loses her child.

TRACKER

Thirteen-year-old John Borne visits his dying grandfather. He finds out that he will be going hunting alone this year and heads out to find a doe. He tracks the doe for three days until the doe lies down in exhaustion. John's touching the wild animal was his way of connecting with death and having a better understanding of losing his grandfather.

WOODSONG

Gary Paulsen trains his dogs and runs his first Iditarod. Written in the first-person present tense, the story of his interactions with his dogs shows Paulsen's skill in writing man-against-nature stories. His picture of the seventeen days of the race is filled with thrilling immediacy.

POPCORN DAYS AND BUTTERMILK NIGHTS

Fourteen-year-old Carley visits Uncle David in northern Minnesota where he finds poverty and love he had never known. Working with hot steel in Uncle David's forge and living with his family of seven children show Carley how survival and happiness come from families and neighbors working together.

DANCING CARL

Thirteen-year-old Willy and his friend observe Carl, a war veteran and alcoholic, who manages an ice rink. One minute, Carl reacts harshly to a model of a B-12 that one of the boys shows Carl. The next minute Carl is helping little children across the ice rink. When a mentally retarded young woman named Helen comes to the rink, Carl helps her with her skates and she and Carl turn onto the ice in a ritualistic dance.

TILTAWHIRL JOHN

Fifteen-year-old Gary feels trapped when his uncle gives him a parcel of land to farm. So he runs away to make his fortune some other way. After working on a beet farm and being denied his wages he is rescued by three carnival performers. He is happy as a carney making $35 a week running the Tiltawhirl, until he witnesses a knife fight between two carneys. He confesses to a policeman that he is a runaway and is sent back to his uncle's farm. He decides he will be a farmer after all.

THE CROSSING

Manuel Bustos plans to steal money so he can afford to cross the river to a better way of life. Alcoholic Sergeant Robert feels as trapped as Manny does. As the sergeant is being killed by three enemies he gives Manny his wallet and Manny runs for the river and a crossing.

NIGHTJOHN

Written in tribute to Sally Hemmings, this story is about an escaped slave who is caught and tortured by his master. In spite of having his toes cut off, he keeps returning to the plantation to teach Sarney, another young slave to read. Nightjohn establishes a school for slaves.

WINTERKILL

The story of an unhappy thirteen-year-old who meets Duda, a policeman who lives by his own rules and sense of justice.

THE ISLAND

Fourteen-year-old Wil Neuton moves with his family from Madison, Wisconsin to a small community called Pinewood in Northern Minnesota. Wil likes to be alone, observing nature and scribbling characterizations in his notebook. His parents are worried about him and hire a psychologist. Wil shares his joy of observing nature with the psychologist. After a fight with a local bully, Wil determines that his island is the ideal place to be. Finally he sees his father sitting on the shore and he rows over and brings him to his island.

FOXMAN is a war veteran and a fox hunter with a terribly scarred face. He rescues the fourteen-year-old narrator of his story, teaches him survival skills, and shares his books with him. His character seems to be based on Paulsen's own experiences in the service and impressions from his visit to the war-torn Philippines when he was young.

UNCLE DAVID is the young narrator's uncle in *Tiltawhirl John*, a forger and father of a loving family in *Popcorn Days and Buttermilk Nights*, and is the old man in *Sentries* who attempts to recapture memories of his youth by splicing a large log and telling folk tales. He represents tradition and stability in Paulsen's stories.

DUDA is a combination of independent characters who lived by their own rules. He is D.J. who was the policeman in *Pilgrimage on a Steel Ride* who saved the fourteen-year-old Gary from turning to a life of crime. He is Foxman who lived a solitary life in northern Minnesota as a hunter and found solace in reading good books, and he is Dancing Carl who tolerated his own scars from the war by helping those less able than himself. He has the strength and singleness of mind that young Gary saw in Sergeant Ryland in *Eastern Sun, Winter Moon*.

CHARLES GODDARD, the fifteen-year-old in *Soldier's Heart* who enlisted in the First Minnesota Volunteers. Charles fights in the Battles of Bull Run, Gettysburg and on the Delaware/Maryland Line. By nineteen, when he returns home, he is no longer young. The experiences of the war prompt his own suicide at twenty-three years of age.

COOKIE, a sled dog, was Paulsen's lead dog and closest friend for over ten years. He tells her story in *Woodsong*, *Winterdance*, *Pilgrimage on a Steel Ride*, and in *My Life in Dog Years*. He dedicated *Puppies, Dogs and Blue Northers* to her. She helped him survive by pulling the team from icy water and from sliding down a snow-packed mountain. She lived to be fourteen years of age and had seven litters. Many of her offspring became lead dogs.

DANCING CARL

ALA Best Book—1983

TRACKER

Society of Midland Authors Book Award—1985

DOGSONG

Newbery Honor—1986, Children's Book of the Year Award, Child Study Association of America—1986, Volunteer State Book Award—1989,ALA Notable and Best Book—1985.

THE CROSSING

ALA Notable Best Book—1987.

HATCHET

Newbery Honor Book—1988, ALA Notable Book—1987. Booklist Editor's Choice citation—1988, Dorothy Canfield Fisher Children's Book Award—1989, Georgia Children's Book Awards—1991, Young Hoosier Book Awards—1991, Iowa Children's Choice Award and Iowa Teen Award—1990, Maud Hart Lovelace Book Award—1990, Flicker Tale Children's Book Award—1990, Ohio Buckeye Children's Book Award—1990, Sequoyah Children and YA Book Awards—1990, Virginia Young Readers Program—1990, Golden Archer Little Archer Awards—1989.

THE ISLAND

ALA Best Book—1988.

VOYAGE OF THE FROG

Parenting Magazine Reading-Magic Award—1990, Teachers' Choice Award from International Reading Association—1990, Best Books of the Year citation from *Learning* Magazine.

THE WINTER ROOM

Newbery Honor Book—1990, Judy Lopez Memorial Award—1990, Parenting Magazine Best Book of the Year—1990, ALA Notable and Best Book—1989.

BOY WHO OWNED THE SCHOOL

Parents' ChoiceAward—1991

THE COOK CAMP

ALA Best Book—1991, *School Library Journal* Best Book of the Year—1991.

THE MONUMENT
ALA Best Book—1991, *School Library Journal* Best Book of the Year—1991.

THE RIVER
IRA/Children's Book Council—1991, *Parents Magazine* Best Book of the Year—1991.

WOODSONG
Booklist Editor's Choice citation—1991, Society of Midland Authors Book Award—1991, Spur Award, Western Writers of America—1991, Minnesota Book Awards—1991.

HAYMEADOW
Spur Award—1993, ALA Notable and Best Book—1992.

DOGTEAM
IRA/Children's Book Council—1994.

HARRIS AND ME: A SUMMER REMEMBERED
Booklist Books for Youth Top of the List citation—1993, ALA Notable and Best book—1993.

NIGHTJOHN
IRA/Children's Book Council—1994, ALA Notable and Best Book—1993.

SISTERS/HERMANAS
Children's Literature Award Finalist, PEN Center USA West—1994.

DOGSONG
Parents' Choice Award, Parents'ChoiceFoundation—1985 Three Newbery Honors, Newbery Award, ALA Notable Books, Western Writers of America Golden Spur Award.

Paulsen, Gary. *Eastern Sun, Winter Moon*. New York: Harcourt Brace Jovanovich, Publishers, 1993.

Paulsen, Gary. "Joys, Fears, and Changes," in Magpies 4, no. 5, (November 1989): 5-10.

Paulsen, Gary. *Pilgrimage on a Steel Ride*. New York: Harcourt Brace and Company, 1997.

Paulsen, Gary. *Puppies, Dogs and Blue Northers: Reflections on being Raised by a Pack of Sled Dogs.*, ills Ruth Wright Paulsen. New York: Harcourt Brace and Company, 1996.

Peters, Stephanie True. *Gary Paulsen*. Meet the Author Series, The Learning Works, Inc., 1999.

Ungermann, Kenneth A. *The Race to Nome*. Sunnyvale, CA: Press North America/Nulbay Associates, Inc., 1963.

Iron Will. Video Pictures, formatted for TV. Distributed by Buena Vista Home Video Dept. CS. Burbank, California 91521. Walt Disney Company, 1944, Director: Charles Haid, Producer: Patrick Palmer and Robert Schwartz.

http://www.garypaulsen.com
[Author Profile]

http://www.iditarod.com/index.shtml
[Iditarod]

http://borg.lib.vt.edu/ejournals/ALAN/fall94/Schmitz.html
["A Writer of his Time" Fall, 1994, The Alan Review. Digital Library and Archives by James A. Schmitz]

http://falcon.jmu.edu/~ramseyil/paulsen.htm.
[Gary Paulsen by Brenda Hoffman and Inez Ramsey]

ELIZABETH PATERRA has taught and written for children and adults for many years. She especially enjoys writing for and being with middle school and secondary students. She received her doctorate in reading education from the University of Maryland. As a children's literature freelance writer her credits include a number of books and articles. She won first prize for picture books for the SCBWI (Mid-Atlantic Region) and two first prizes for children's one-act plays for the Maryland Writers Association. She lives on Maryland's Eastern Shore with her husband, two children, and their Cairn terrier, Mickey.